SOLD OUT

MY JOURNEY TO A MORE INTIMATE
RELATIONSHIP WITH GOD

ISBN 978-0-6152-1680-5

This is for you, Lord

Thank You

For Loving Me

Acknowledgements
To my two beautiful children, Tommie and Jalisa;
my sisters, every one of you including my wonderful
sister-friends and my sisters in Christ; and to
Daddy, Mama, and Earl
the angels who gave me wings,
I love you and I thank you for your support.
God bless you all.

Table of Contents

Introduction

One of the most obvious, but important truths I have learned in my walk with God is that life is a journey, and heaven is the destination. God created man as a free will agent to serve him by choice. Adam and Eve had the same choice that we have today: obey him and live or reject him and die. **In choosing to disobey God by eating of the tree of the knowledge of good and evil, Adam and Eve sinned, suffering immediate and dire consequences.**

1. They lost their Godly innocence and gained sin consciousness.
2. This caused them to be aware of their nakedness and they became ashamed and tried to cover themselves. *Genesis 4:7*
3. They experienced spiritual death: *for the wages of sin is death. Romans 6:23.* **The soul that sinneth, it shall die.** *Ezekiel 18:4*
4. God drove them out of the Garden before they could partake of the tree of life and live forever in their sinful state. *Genesis 5:22*
5. They brought the curse of sin and its penalty ; death, on all mankind. *1Corinthians 15:22*
   As a result, we are all born in sin and therefore; spiritually dead:
   " *Behold I was shapen in iniquity and in sin did my mother conceive me.Psalm:51*
6. Just as one man, Adam, brought sin on all mankind through his disobedience, One man, Jesus Christ brought salvation to all mankind through his obedience. *1Corinthians 15:22*

God does not wink at sin. His very character demands that justice be satisfied. The wages of sin is death, and this death penalty is still in effect for all who reject Christ. God sent Jesus to carry out his plan of salvation because Jesus Christ lived out the innocent sinless life that Adam and Eve could not, and then he willingly obeyed God by taking the death penalty upon himself. His innocent blood satisfied what justice demanded. *The soul that sinneth it shall die.* God accepts the blood of Jesus as the acceptable substitute for your sins and mine; because he died, we don't have to. When Jesus died on the cross he uttered the words; "It is finished." This meant that God's plan of salvation was complete. Now any man who will understand and believe that Jesus died for their sins can be saved from the curse of sin and the death penalty. Though they were born spiritually dead, they can be spiritually reborn through faith in Jesus Christ. This is what is meant by the term, 'born again Christian.'

We begin our journey the day we give our lives to Christ and are spiritually reborn. With the help of the Holy Spirit we grow and mature in Christ and fulfill God's purpose for our lives. We come to the end of this life, and we pass into the next, where we inherit eternal life through faith in Jesus Christ: *"For God so loved the world that he gave his only begotten son, that whosoever believest on his shall not perish, but they shall have eternal life." John 3:16* Today, we are faced with the same choice as Adam and Eve; accept him and live eternally in paradise, or reject him and face death and eternal torment in hell. We are still free will agents. God will not force salvation upon us; he simply offers it to any person who is willing to accept it. **Here is the key to God's Plan of Salvation; Acceptance.** If I was to stand before you offering a one hundred dollar bill, it becomes yours the moment you walked up, took it from my hand and accepted it as yours. I can offer it to you all day, but the benefits of owning that one hundred dollar bill can never be enjoyed by you until you accept it. It will not happen by osmosis. Acknowledging the existence of the money does not give you the same benefits of owning it; there must be a decision on your part to accept it as your own. To put it simply, **there has to be a moment in life when you consciously and willingly accept Jesus as your personal savior and surrender your life to him. I hope this book will encourage you do just that and I pray that as you read about my journey, it will inspire you to begin your own journey to a more intimate relationship with God.**

My Journey

When I think of how I first began this journey of faith, it almost seems like a fluke. Here I was twenty two years old, having 'grown up' in church, and pretty sure that I was a fairly decent Christian. Then one day, I think in a laundromat, I picked up a pamphlet that caught my attention entitled, "Are You Saved?" I really didn't like the term 'saved.' I associated it with those snooty holy rollers from my school days, who wore long dresses and said 'praise the Lord' after every sentence. Still, I opened it quite smugly, thinking that it had been left there for some unchurched person to 'find Jesus.'

But as I read, I realized that I could not remember ever confessing with my mouth nor believing in my heart that Jesus died for my sins. I had heard this gospel preached in church all of my life, but it had never been presented to me in such a personal way. As I sat there reading, I began to remember all the terrible things I had done, said, thought, and felt even though I was supposed to be a Christian.

My heart filled with godly sorrow as I thought about the punishment I deserved, versus the blessings and protection that I had been given. Nights when I had been out doing everything I was bad enough to do, riding home in the car with a drunk driver, and still making it home safely.

More near misses, and close calls than I cared to think about. But God had kept me through it all. And finally I understood why.

Because he loved me.

When I was so messed up that I didn't even love myself, God loved me. He loved me so much that he sent his son Jesus Christ to pay the penalty for my sins so that I would not have to. All I had to do was believe this in my heart and confess it with my mouth. The pamphlet guided me through the sinner's prayer, and I was saved right there in that laundromat.

That was almost thirty years ago, and through the years, God has continued to draw me closer to him each day through his lovingkindess. I love him because he first loved me and today I am completely sold out to Jesus.

This book is a compilation of some of the messages I have preached and written during my ten years in ministry. It traces my journey from a place of 'polite' intimacy with a God that I mainly feared and respected, (I still do), to a place of total surrender and 'raw' intimacy with the God I have grown to **love with all that is in me.**

I have written it for one purpose; to reach you dear reader with the love of Jesus Christ. My prayer is first that you will hear, understand and accept the message of salvation through faith in Jesus Christ and become sold out to Jesus.

For those who have already given their lives to Jesus, I pray that these messages will bless and edify you in your walk with God and help you reach a place of deeper intimacy with Him as you learn to trust and surrender your life to Him. I ask that the minute you finish reading it, you will partner with me in my endeavor to reach people with the message of God's love by sharing this book with someone else and asking them to do the same.

Understanding The Conversion Experience

Luke 22:31-32 reads: *And the Lord said, Simon, Simon, behold, Satan hath desired to have you, that he may sift you as wheat: But I have prayed for thee, that thy faith fail not: and when thou art converted, strengthen thy brethren*

I must confess that when I first read this, I was a bit puzzled. What did Jesus mean when he said "When though art converted?" I mean, wasn't he speaking to **Peter**? Simon Peter ? The man who was the very first to be called of the twelve disciples.

The only one to ever walk on water . The first one to recognize Jesus as the son of God.

That Peter?

Jesus was indeed speaking to that very Peter.

You see, before Peter could ever preach that first sermon after the coming of the Holy Spirit in which three thousand souls were added to the church, or before he would become that rock to whom Jesus referred when He said, *"Upon this rock, I will build my church."*

Before Peter could ever really be used by God, he had to be converted.

If we are really going to fulfill the will of God for our lives, and be the anointed vessels he has created us to be, then, like Peter, **we too, must have a conversion experience.**

My sister Tracy is one of the most honest people I know. If you were to ask her if she has been converted, her answer to that question would be,

*"Converted? Yeah I'm converted! What you mean have I been converted? Sure I have. Wait a minute. What does **converted** mean?"*

The biblical word for conversion means "turning". Think of a person who is going along a road and suddenly realizes that he or she is on the wrong track. They will never reach the destination if they continue in that direction. So the person 'turns," or 'is converted." He or she ceases to go in the wrong direction and begins going in the right one.

Conversion changes the direction of one's course of life from the wrong way to the right way, the way that God wants. The result of true conversion is a **closer walk with God**.

Conversion is not only that decisive act in which we as sinners turn away from sin in genuine repentance and accept the salvation that Christ offers. There is a deeper aspect to the conversion experience. The decision to turn only begins the process of true conversion.

I believe there are three very necessary elements required for a conversion experience: 1. **True repentance**, 2. **A heart for the things of God**, and 3. A **consuming passion to seek and fulfill the will of God for your life.**

The bible records many, many incidents of conversions, including the dramatic experience of the Apostle **Paul on the Damascus road**, but I believe the most compelling example is that of Simon Peter. Let us examine it more closely:

And the Lord said, Simon, Simon, behold, Satan hath desired to have you, that he may sift you as wheat: 32: But I have prayed for thee, that thy faith fail not: and when thou art converted, strengthen thy brethren. 33: And he said unto him, Lord, I am ready to go with thee, both into prison, and to death. 34: And he said, I tell thee, Peter, the cock shall not crow this day, before that thou shalt thrice deny that thou

knowest me. (Luke 22:31-34)

Within the context of the conversion experience, we can say that **at this point, Peter was like the example of the person who is traveling on the wrong road.** Only at this point he still has not realized that he is on the wrong road. He thinks that he is able to stand against the enemy under his own power instead of relying on the power of God to sustain him.

One of the first things that we as Christians need to understand is that Jesus knows us better than we know ourselves. Often when we are new in the faith, we have a zeal but it is not according to knowledge. Because of this, God sometimes has to protect us from our own foolish impulses.

Most of us fondly remember how it was when we first came to a saving knowledge of Jesus Christ. I was all fired up, ready to save the world. I was just in love with the Lord. I had no idea that my flesh was not saved. I was like a lot of new Christians, who thought they were Super Saints. It's funny how we can't recognize how foolish we are at this stage, but when we get past it, we can easily see it in other people. **And so can Jesus**. It is as though he were saying "Yes Peter, I know you think you really mean you are ready to go all the way. but trust me, you are not. And you are going to find out that you are not in just a little while.

Our story continues :

54: Then took they him, and led him, and brought him into the high priest's house. And Peter followed afar off. 55: And when they had kindled a fire in the midst of the hall, and were set down together, Peter sat down among them. 56: But a certain maid beheld him as he sat by the fire, and earnestly looked upon him, and said, This man was also with him. 57: And he denied him, saying, Woman, I know him not. 58: And after a little while another saw him, and said, Thou art also of them. And Peter said, Man, I am not. 59: And about the space of one hour after another confidently affirmed, saying, Of a truth this fellow also was with him: for he is a Galilaean. 60: And Peter said, Man, I know not what thou sayest. And immediately, while he yet spake, the cock crew. 61: And the Lord turned, and looked upon Peter. And Peter remembered the word of the Lord, how he had said unto him, Before the cock crow, thou shalt deny me thrice. 62: And Peter went out, and wept bitterly. This may have been the darkest hour of Peter's life. But it was also one of the most important when it comes to his conversion. It was the moment of **true repentance.** The moment when he felt the Holy Spirit prick his conscience and he began to feel godly sorrow in his heart. <u>And he wept.</u>

Few things can make you feel true Godly sorrow for your sins like the day your eyes become open to the fact that while you were yet in that sin, God had mercy on your soul.

I don't know about you, but when I think about where I was and what I was doing when God's grace found me;

I think about how many close calls I had while I was out there doing everything that I was big enough to do and how many horrible consequences I could have suffered;

I think about how merciful God was to give me the time and space to come to repentance;

I think about all those times even now when I miss the mark how he covers me and keeps me from coming to open shame.

Like Peter, my heart breaks with sorrow sometimes when I realize that I have hurt and offended the God who has never done anything to me but love me completely, and unconditionally just as I am. <u>This is true repentance.</u>

But Jesus was not though until there was a complete and full restoration of Peter's soul.

14: This is now the third time that Jesus showed himself to his disciples, after that he was risen from the dead. 15: So when they had dined, Jesus saith to Simon Peter, Simon, son of Jonas, lovest thou me more than these? He saith unto him, Yea, Lord; thou knowest that I love thee. He saith unto him, Feed my lambs. 16: He saith to him again the second time, Simon, son of Jonas, lovest thou me? He saith unto him, Yea, Lord;

thou knowest that I love thee. He saith unto him,

Feed my sheep. 17: He saith unto him the third

time, Simon, son of Jonas, lovest thou me? Peter

was grieved because he said unto him the third

time, Lovest thou me? And he said unto him,

Lord, thou knowest all things; thou knowest that I

love thee. Jesus saith unto him, Feed my sheep.

God's grace is so amazing. Now that Peter was humbled and brought entirely under grace, he realized he had no strength to stand on his own, and he finally understood his complete and utter dependence on the Lord. Peter's conversion caused him to turn away from prideful self- dependence and begin to truly follow Jesus with all his heart. **A heart that was now fully converted; ready and willing to concern himself with the things and people of God.**

Peter's conversion was now complete. He spent the rest of his life in a **passionate relentless pursuit to fulfill the commission that Jesus had given him to 'strengthen his brethren' and 'feed his sheep'.**

All those Sundays when I came to church, sang in the choir, and even showed up in Sunday school every now and then, sometimes with the scent of the world still on my breath and the sinful desires still in my heart, **God had mercy**. I was in Church and on my way to hell, but **God had mercy**. My name was written on the church roll, but my heart did not belong to the Lord, but **God had mercy**. I had never had a true conversion experience. I was traveling; but I was on the wrong road. The prideful self-dependent road that said I could make it in through church work and being a good person.

I was an insufferable **goody two shoes, and it had blinded me to my true spiritual condition**. In reality, **I was rotten.** I had done, thought, and said some terrible things in my life, and those who are honest enough to admit know that at some point they too have missed the mark.

<u>I was sitting in church on my way to hell.</u>

In order to experience **true conversion**, you have to understand that there are **immediate and dire consequences to sin.**

Heaven is real my friend.

So is hell.

For me, conversion came from understanding the reality of hell, and knowing that without God, I was on my way there. It came from knowing that in accepting Christ as my Savior, I had just escaped eternal torment , and the only reason I was blessed enough to do so before dying in my sins was because of **God's grace and mercy.**

That's the beauty of grace.

God gives us time and space to repent

and accept the salvation that he offers through

Jesus Christ. But some of us just continue in sin

because his grace is so abundant.

Let me assure you, **you don't want to go to hell**,

and the blood of Jesus Christ is your only escape:

Without the shedding of blood there is no remission

[of sins]. Hebrews 9:22

Jesus has only pure and sinless blood that is an

acceptable sacrifice for our sins.

Because he died, we don't have to. (John 3:16).

The moment we accept Jesus as our savior,

some wonderful things happen:

1. We are immediately released from the curse of
   sin and its penalty; death. We are born again
   and become new creatures in him, *2Corinthisans*
   5:17. At the moment of our confession, God

begins the lifelong process of transforming us into the image of Christ.

It doesn't mean we won't sin, it means we are covered by the blood of Jesus and God accepts this as the atonement for confessed sin.

2. We regain our right to the tree of life. *Revelation 22:14*

3. We become heirs and joint heirs with Christ. Every thing he promised becomes ours to claim. *Romans 8:17*

4. Our names are written in the Lamb's Book of Life. *Luke 10:20*

5. Death loses its sting. 1Corinthians *15:55-57*. It no longer becomes something for us to dread because we know the joy that awaits us on the other side. At the moment of death we are ushered into the very presence of God. In the words of the apostle Paul, to be absent from the

body, is to be present with the Lord.

2Corinthians 5:8

God's plan of salvation is to reconcile man unto himself through the blood of Jesus so that we may again enjoy all the things He has prepared for us. We cannot even imagine the wonderful things God has in store for those who love him and give their lives to Jesus. *1Corinthians 2:9*

But if I were you I wouldn't let another day pass just skating by on grace. I wouldn't play games of chance with my life. Today could be the day tha you know, that you know, **that you know**, that if you left this world today, you would be safe in his arms.

<u>You can be saved right here and right now.</u>

When I was saved, I was alone in the presence of God with only this promise from God to guide me: *That if thou shalt* **confess with thy mouth** *the Lord Jesus and shall* **believe in thine heart** *that God raised him from the dead, thou shalt be saved. Romans 10:9*

We are saved by grace through faith in Christ. It is just that simple.

If you know deep in your heart that you are not saved, and you can feel the Holy Spirit tugging at your heart, I implore you to lift your heart unto the Lord and receive the his gift of NEW life in Jesus Christ.

Pray this simple prayer:

"Heavenly Father,
I believe in you and that your word is true.
I confess with my mouth that Jesus Christ is
the Son of the living God and that he died on the
cross so that I may now have forgiveness for my sins
and inherit eternal life.
Be merciful unto me, a sinner and forgive my sins.
I believe in my heart that you,
Lord God, raised Jesus from the dead,
and today, I accept Jesus as my personal savior.
Jesus, I invite you to come into my heart. I give you
my life and I ask you to take full control
from this moment on;
I pray this in the name of Jesus Christ."
Amen.

Knowing Your Purpose

Once we are saved, our immediate goal should be
to **learn God's purpose for our lives**.

Everyone has a purpose, and that purpose is
seldom singular. Too often we decide on one
purpose such as singing, ministry, parenting, etc,
but this may not always be the case. I believe our
purpose is closely tied to our times and seasons
and may gradually change depending on what
season of life we may be in.

For example, in one season our purpose may be to marry, (in the Lord), give birth, and raise godly children who grow up to be men and women of God. However, once those children are adults and we have fulfilled that part of God's purpose for our lives, that does not mean God is finished with us. He can and will use our gifts and talents for his purpose in the earth no matter how old or young we may be. Whether we are called to many years of divinely ordained study and research in order to write, create, or discover something that will cure, heal, uplift, or enlighten humanity, or just to teach Sunday school, take in a foster child, or be a light in our workplace, as long as we are alive, God can use us. Like the apostle Paul on the Damascus road, our prayer should continually be: *Lord, what wilt thou have me to do?* (Act 9:6).

Our mission in this journey we call life should be to fulfill our purpose and walk out God's will for our lives.

The seed of divine purpose exists within every person. But too many of us fail to fulfill our calling. Salvation is God's gift to us. Answering his call to serve his purpose for our lives should be our gift to him. The question is simple. If you are not walking in your purpose, what is there to give meaning and purpose to your life? God gives us all of the gifts, talents, and abilities we need to fulfill our purpose. I cannot say this enough.

Our gifts and talents are not for us.

They are not given to entertain our family, friends, and church members. They are not given to earn us fame and fortune, though that may come to some. Our gifts and talents were given to us so that we might glorify God, and edify his people. The manner in which we accomplish this is up to us.

God offers us the guidance of his word and the Holy Spirit to help; the faith and works are up to us. When our purpose in this life has been fulfilled, we are then ready to pass from our earthly life to eternal life.

Understanding Your Enemy

The Christian Journey is not a skip through the park; there is an enemy who wants to steal, kill, and destroy us. Make no mistake about it. Your enemy the devil is like a roaring lion, seeking whom he may devour. *1Peter 5:8* As my mother would say, "And he aint playing!"

But too many of us are. We entertain too many things and people who have been sent to us 'on assignment' to do one of three things:

1. **Steal** our joy through trials, doubt, fear, distractions, hardships, persecution, etc. (Please read the Chapter on **Stolen Joy**).

2. **Kill** us before we fulfill our purpose (through temporary weaknesses of the flesh, temptation with worldly pleasures that have deadly consequences such as drugs and hazardous relationships, and then kill us in our sin. When we willingly step outside of the ark of safety (Jesus Christ) we become vulnerable to the enemy.

3. **Destroy** our witness by leading us into temptation then exposing us to the world. (Read the story of David and Bathsheba).

Always remember that there are two ways to overcome the enemy:

*And they overcame him by **the blood of the Lamb** and by **the word of their testimony**. Rev. (12:11)*

Keeping Your Joy

The enemy knows that the blood of Jesus protects our lives, and covers our confessed sins, but sometimes, we allow him to literally steal our joy. Losing your joy is one of the worst things that can happen to a child of God, *for the joy of the LORD is your strength (Neh. 8:10).*

A few years ago, I was having dinner with someone who would eventually become very important to me.

Suddenly he broke away from the usual 'date' chatter and asked me, **"Are you happy?"**

I was taken aback by the question, mainly because I had never really thought about it. I stared at him for a moment, unsure of how much of an answer he really wanted. My answer surprised even me.

"Happiness is such a subjective term, I replied. "There are so many things that most people depend on to make them feel 'happy'. I paused for a moment, not sure I could find the right words to make him understand. Then it came to me.

"In my heart", I told him, "there is a deep abiding joy. There are time when it just bubbles inside me, and sometimes it overflows. No matter what is going on in my life, and even when I am not particularly 'happy', I feel this joy.

It is really hard to explain and probably even harder to understand, but to me, it is one of the best parts of my journey."

I didn't realize it then, but **what I was describing was the joy of the Lord.**

When I search my memory, I cannot recall when it came to me, or how long it had been with me. It just kind of overtook me like the time when I was working as a school nurse. I was assigned to a middle school where I was a familiar face to many of the students, some of whom were active in their school extracurricular activities.

One Saturday as I was driving past the school, I realized that I had driven into and was about to be overtaken by their homecoming motorcade. The street was blocked, so I had no choice but to pull over to the side of the road and wait it out.

As the motorcade passed my little car, I began to hear my name being called. Suddenly, I was inundated with candy and goodies that seemed to be falling from the sky. Some of my favorite students had recognized their nurse and were directing their throws toward me. The bag of goodies I left with was an unexpected but very welcome perk of working with these children.

The joy of the Lord will often overtake a believer in much the same way. As he or she walks with and draws closer to God, at some point, when it is least expected joy takes root in the soul growing sweeter by the day until it literally fills to overflowing.

As believers, joy in the Lord is a sustaining force in our lives. It can keep us going when nothing else will because it is joy that helps us to keep our eyes on Jesus and his promises rather than our circumstances.

~ 40 ~

It is joy that keeps us with a song in our hearts and praise on our lips, even when to those around us, our world seems to be falling apart.

A few years ago my mother who had been confined to a wheelchair after she lost her legs to diabetes, accidentally fell from her wheelchair and hit her head.

The blow caused massive intracranial bleeding, and we watched in horror as she slipped into a coma. Within twenty-four hours, she was dead. At her deathbed, my oldest brother Matthew tried to be strong as always. while my eight sisters and I stood weeping and covering mother's face with tearful kisses until I thought our hearts would break. We usually found such strength in each other, but being newly orphaned, we were desolate. I suddenly felt led to ask my older sister Esther, to pray and thank God for our time with mother.

As she began her earnest prayer, the glory of the Lord filled the room, and soon we were loudly shouting and praising God for the wonderful gift of time he had given us with mother. Even the nurses and hospital staff were drawn to the sound of our joyful praises as God turned our mourning into joy. Each time I think of mother's passing, I am forced to remember that day, and the joy I felt then sustains me even now.

The first principle of real joy is that it is constant: it will flow in spite of and in the midst of any circumstance. Nehemiah 8: 10 tells us that the joy of the Lord is our strength. By refusing to believe the lies of the enemy and choosing to give praise and glory to God in all things, we rob the enemy of his victory. We get the victory instead, and each victory helps us to win the next.

When unthinkable things happen to us as children of God, joy is what keeps us dancing, shouting, and giving God glory even in the midst of our pain. When all hell breaks loose and nothing is going right, joy is what gives us the strength to get out of bed on a Sunday morning, put on our clothes, and run to the house of the Lord

Unspeakable Joy

As God takes us from glory to glory, our joy increases until we get to what I believe is the highest level of joy that can be experienced on this side of glory: unspeakable joy. When the Lord allowed David to bring the Ark of the covenant to Jerusalem, after one failed attempt that resulted in Uzzah's death, his joy was so full that *he danced before the Lord with all of his might.(2nd Samuel 6:14).* He had unspeakable joy.

Unspeakable joy is often birthed through deliverance from great trials and suffering. When you've been through enough times, and been delivered enough times, and seen the power of God operating in your life enough times, every round takes you a little higher, and draws you a little closer until after a while you are so filled with the joy of the Lord that you can't even tell it.

After that, there is no longer a need to hope and pray that things will get better, now you know for sure that they will. You don't just wonder if you are going to make it; now you know that you will. You don't have to wonder what God' s going to do; you can just look at what he's already done!

And just looking at what God has already done is reason enough to give him the praise in advance for what he is going to do.

Unspeakable joy will have folks thinking 'she must be crazy!. Think about it. If everybody in the church knows that Sister Do-good's husband has left, her car's been repossessed, and her phone is disconnected, yet every Sunday, she's up dancing and shouting and declaring how good God is, some folks will think she is either in denial or about to have a nervous breakdown. But she is simply an illustration of **the second principle of real joy: The world (and its circumstances) can't give it, and the world can't take it away.**

It should be clear now that joy is something every believer must have. It can sustain us when nothing else will. Joy is an unexpected but cherished gift from God to every believer and it must be guarded. There are so many things that can come against us and cause us to lose our joy.

When we do, we are like a bird with a broken wing; hampered in our ability to soar above our circumstances into that blessed place of peace and joy in the Lord. I believe that there are two situations when a believer may find himself without joy: when it is **lost**, and when it is **stolen**.

Lost Joy

Lost joy is usually the believer's fault. Unconfessed sin or rebelliousness can cause us to lose our joy. David's encounter with Bathsheba is, I believe, a classic case of joy lost through sin and rebelliousness.

2 Samuel 11:2-26 is the account of David and Bathsheba.:

2 And it came to pass in an eveningtide, that David arose from off his bed, and walked upon the roof of the king's house: and from the roof he saw a woman washing herself; and the woman was very beautiful to look upon. 3 And David sent and enquired after the woman. And one said, Is not this Bathsheba, the daughter of Eliam, the wife of Uriah the Hittite? 4 And David sent messengers, and took her; and she came in unto him, and he lay with her; for she was purified from her uncleanness: and she returned unto her house. 5 And the woman conceived, and sent and told David, and said, I am with child. 6 And David sent to Joab, saying, Send me Uriah the Hittite. And Joab sent Uriah to David. 7 And when Uriah was come unto him, David demanded of him how Joab did, and how the people did, and how the war prospered. 8 And David said to Uriah, Go down to thy house, and wash thy feet. And Uriah departed out of the king's house, and there followed him a mess of meat from the king. 9 But Uriah slept at the door of the king's house with all the servants of his lord, and went not down to his house. 10 And when they had told David, saying, Uriah went not down *unto his house, David said unto Uriah, Camest thou*

not from thy journey? why then didst thou not go

down unto thine house? 11 And Uriah said unto

David, The ark, and Israel, and Judah, abide in

tents; and my lord Joab, and the servants of my

lord, are encamped in the open fields; shall I then go

into mine house, to eat and to drink, and to lie with

my wife? as thou livest, and as thy soul liveth, I will

not do this thing. 12 And David said to Uriah, Tarry

here to day also, and to morrow I will let thee

depart. So Uriah abode in Jerusalem that day, and

the morrow. 13 And when David had called him, he

did eat and drink before him; and he made him

drunk: and at even he went out to lie on his bed with

the servants of his lord, but went not down to his

house. 14 And it came to pass in the morning, that

David wrote a letter to Joab, and sent it by the hand

of Uriah. 15 And he wrote in the letter, saying, Set

ye Uriah in the forefront of the hottest battle, and

retire ye from him, that he may be smitten, and die. 16 And it came to pass, when Joab observed the city, that he assigned Uriah unto a place where he knew that valiant men were. 17 And the men of the city went out, and fought with Joab: and there fell some of the people of the servants of David; and Uriah the Hittite died also. 18 Then Joab sent and told David all the things concerning the war; 19 And charged the messenger, saying, When thou hast made an end of telling the matters of the war unto the king, 20 And if so be that the king's wrath arise, and he say unto thee, Wherefore approached ye so nigh unto the city when ye did fight? knew ye not that they would shoot from the wall? 21 Who smote Abimelech the son of Jerubbesheth? did not a woman cast a piece of a millstone upon him from the wall, that he died in Thebez? why went ye nigh the wall? then say thou, Thy servant Uriah the Hittite is dead also. 22

22 So the messenger went, and came and shewed David all that Joab had sent him for. 23 And the messenger said unto David, Surely the men prevailed against us, and came out unto us into the field, and we were upon them even unto the entering of the gate. 24 And the shooters shot from off the wall upon thy servants; and some of the king's servants be dead, and thy servant Uriah the Hittite is dead also. 25 Then David said unto the messenger, Thus shalt thou say unto Joab, Let not this thing displease thee, for the sword devoureth one as well as another: make thy battle more strong against the city, and overthrow it: and encourage thou him. 26 And when the wife of Uriah heard that Uriah her husband was dead, she mourned for her husband. 27 And when the mourning was past, David sent and fetched her to his house, and she became his wife, and bare him a son. But the thing that David had done displeased the LORD.

This story sounds incredible, but it is nonetheless true;

Not only did David sleep with another man's wife, but he also set him up to be killed in battle and then married her!

Even though he was a man after God's own heart, the things David had done were greatly displeasing to the Lord. <u>David suffered greatly for his sin and even after he confessed and repented, there were still consequences and repercussions.</u>

David lost his joy in the Lord and in Psalms 51, he prays for God to, *restore unto me the joy of thy salvation.(Psalm51:14)*

Through a trap set by the enemy, David was lured into sin, and the enemy is still setting traps and snares for unsuspecting believers today.

His goal is to entice you to sin and then keep you there until your are so caught up that you feel there is no escape.

My mother used to call this the *"can't-help-its."* When people are infected with this, they start saying really stupid things, like,

'I know this is wrong, but if feels so good. I just can't help it !'

The problem is that everything that's good **to** you is not necessarily good **for** you. After a little while of enjoying that thing that is so good to, you reach a point where it no longer feels so good. In fact, you become unable to feel anything except **guilt** and **condemnation.**

You start to believe that you have done so much wrong for so long that God could not possibly love or use you anymore.

You may become too ashamed to pray, or when you do pray the guilt and condemnation will not go away. Some people even say that they can no longer feel God in their hearts.

Anyone who has ever been caught up in something like this can readily tell you; **It's a bad feeling to love God, and want to be in his favor, and yet be all caught up in something you know is not pleasing to him.** The apostle Paul describes this dilemma in the book of Romans:

21 I find then a law, that, when I would do good, evil is present with me. 22 For I delight in the law of God after the inward man: 23 But I see another law in my members, warring against the law of my mind, and bringing me into captivity to the law of sin which is in my members. 24 O wretched man that I am! who shall deliver me from the body of this death? (Romans 7:21-24)

Sin and rebelliousness may bring fleeting pleasure to your flesh, but in the end, you feel miserable. You become filled with anger and disgust at yourself. You lose your joy in the Lord, and inevitably, you become deeply depressed.

Stolen Joy

Stolen joy, on the other hand, is not always directly the fault of the believer. Consider God's servant, Job. The bible says that Job was a perfect and upright man who feared God and eschewed evil.

1 There was a man in the land of Uz, whose name was Job; and that man was perfect and upright, and one that feared God, and eschewed evil.(Job 1:1)

But Job's joy was stolen through circumstances beyond his control:

9 Then Satan answered the LORD, and said, Doth Job fear God for nought? 10 Hast not thou made an hedge about him, and about his house, and about all that he hath on every side? thou hast blessed the work of his hands, and his substance is increased in the land. 11 But put forth thine hand now, and touch all that he hath, and he will curse thee to thy face. 12 And the LORD said unto Satan, Behold, all that he hath is in thy power; only upon himself put not forth thine hand. So Satan went forth from the presence of the LORD. (Job 1:9-12)

Sometimes if the enemy cannot lure you into sin, he will attack your family, your finances, your relationships, and even your body (sometimes all at the same time). His goal is to cause you to become so discouraged that you begin to entertain his lies and doubt God's word.

During these attacks, some people even have the audacity to get angry with God. The very weapon that can give them victory is stolen from them by the enemy; as a result, instead of getting victory through praise, they cry, whine, and complain. The doubt and despair that result will sometimes cause the believer to lose his joy and become depressed and broken.

Depression: The Result of Lost or Stolen Joy

Whether you have lost your joy through sin and rebellion, or had it stolen through no fault of your own, the result is still the same; the debilitating paralysis of **depression and brokenness.** Most dictionaries define depression as a disorder marked by sadness, inactivity, difficulty in thinking and feelings of dejection. To be depressed is to literally be low in spirit.

It may have many physical manifestations, but I believe it is a **spiritual** condition.

What does it feel like to be depressed?

In my experience, and in those of the many people that I have spoken with or counseled on the matter, there are many different ways depression can manifest itself, but most of them describe the feeling as a deep sense of sadness alternating with anxiety, which often results from a loss or traumatic incident which may have happened months or even years ago. Even so, you cannot get past it; you just know that nothing and no one can make you feel better. **You are in a place of complete and utter brokenness**.

Some years ago, I met a wonderful man. We fell in love and we dreamed of a life together. I cannot recall a happier time in my life. But one day he got sick. I took him to the hospital and when I left him all was well. When I kissed him goodbye, he was smiling and watching the World Series.

But when I arrived at the hospital the next evening, he seemed to have taken a turn for the worst. He could barely speak above a whisper, but he clearly asked me for water. As I helped him sit up to take a sip of the water, he collapsed in my arms.

He had suffered a massive stroke.

My friend never regained consciousness, and within two days he was dead.

Worse than the pain,

 worse than the suffering,

Worse than the months of mind-numbing grief,

Worse than anything else about this experience was the <u>feeling that I would never, ever be all right again</u>.

I was broken.

That's what depression does

It makes you feel so bad that you want to die.

Then Satan begins to tell you the lie that you would be better off dead.

Like me, you may be too scared of hell to commit suicide, but still you want to die because you just want an end to the pain.

If you are a believer there may also be an overwhelming sense of guilt. Even after repenting, you still feel that what you have done is so bad that God cannot possibly forgive you or love you anymore. You may feel that you are being punished for some past sin, and that you deserve it.

And when you reach that place of brokenness, like me, one of the hardest things for you to understand and believe is that God is with you. But, I never would have made it, if God had not been with me. Through it all, God never left my side, and guess what? He will never leave nor forsake **you** either.

Because you have prayed for relief without success, you become convinced that God has turned his back on you and no longer hears or answers your prayers. You feel too ashamed to tell people that you need help, especially if you are the kind of person who people look at as some kind of super saint, so in all of this, you suffer silently and alone.

You begin to draw away from friends and family. You may sleep a lot, or worse, begin to use drugs or alcohol

Sometimes you may find yourself getting in or clinging to an ungodly relationship just so you won't have to be alone **After a while you become pretty sure that you are going crazy.** All the while, you may be still going to church, lifting up holy hands, dancing and shouting. When folks ask you how you are doing, you smile and tell them fine, **when you are actually dying inside**.

Here is where some of us remain for weeks, months, or even years. We let depression come uninvited, and stay much too long. This is always dangerous because it can and often will lead to a profound **clinical depression**, a serious medical condition which can be **deadly**.

A Warning About Clinical Depression

Clinical depression is caused by a chemical imbalance in the brain sometimes brought on by a stressful or traumatic incident. I believe all depressive episodes have the potential to lead to clinical depression, and if you suspect that this is happening to you, seek medical help immediately! **I did**.

For those who feel that there is something 'unspiritual' about seeking medical help for depression, think about this. If seeking medical attention for diabetes, or high blood pressure does not make you feel like you don't have enough faith, then you should not have a problem seeking help for depression. <u>All of these conditions are caused by chemical imbalances.</u>

As women and men of God, we can find the time to attend to everybody's needs except our own. We need to start **<u>attending to ourselves</u>** , and one important way we can do that is to learn to holler when we get hit. One of the biggest lies of the enemy to a believer going through depression is that he or she is alone, and nobody will understand what they are going through.

If you think that anything you have read here describes your experience, I implore you; **pick up the phone, call a loved one, and tell them what you are feeling.** You may be surprised to discover that at some point they may have dealt with depression either personally, or through someone they are close to.

When my friend suddenly died, I was devastated. The period of grief and depression that followed is one of the darkest periods of my life. Months after most people thought I should have been better, I was still numb with grief. Help came through a co-worker who'd had a similar experience when her mother died. She insisted on making me an appointment to see her pastor, a licensed counselor. I credit this wonderful man of God with putting me on the road to recovery. It may have never happened if I had not confided in that co-worker.

The Way Out of Depression: Through

When it comes to depression, sometimes, the only way out is through. Some things you have just got to go through. Depression is never sudden and neither is getting over it. You've got to trust God and just walk it on out. The problem is that instead of going through depression, we want to set up camp.

As I lay weeping on my bed after my friend died, my world was broken into a million pieces. I felt like I just could not go on.

But I remember my sister Esther calling me that next Sunday morning.

"Get up" she told me, "Wash your face, put on your clothes and make your way to the house of the Lord."

I cried through my shower.

I cried while I was getting dressed.

I cried while I was driving to the church.

I cried when I got there.

But God had his angels there in the form of my sisters. Esther, Cherry, and Tracy all gathered around me and led me to my pastor, Rev. Harry Pugh, who took my hand and prayed for me with such urgency and fervor that I could feel my strength returning. Tears of sorrow became tears of genuine thanksgiving and praise to God for allowing me the privilege of loving and being loved by such a wonderful man.

When I left service that Sunday, I knew I was going to be all right. My victory came through my praise. And so will yours. **Never lose your praise!**

Going through may be painful, but remember, God sets the limits. That which you cannot bear, he will not allow.

No matter what the situation, God will be with you.

Sometimes he will help carry your burden;

sometimes he will carry **you;**

either way, you will get through it!

The good news is that you don't have to go through depression, brokenness, and fiery trials alone.

The Word tells us that God will be with us in whatever we go through:

When thou passest through the waters, I will be with thee; and through the rivers, they shall not overflow thee: when thou walkest through the fire, thou shalt not be burned; neither shall the flame kindle upon thee. (Isaiah 43:2).

Those who pray to be healed of depression should remember this: you didn't just wake up depressed; there was a process involved that took time. Likewise, some people don't always just wake up and walk in healing.

Jesus himself said in some situations, deliverance can only be achieved, **but by prayer and fasting.** *(Matthew 17:21).*

After weeks, months, or years of listening to the devil's lies, there are strongholds that must be pulled down. There are ungodly thoughts that exalt themselves against the knowledge of God that must be cast down. Your mind must be renewed so that any future attempts to attack you are met with God's word. The real key to deliverance is trust;

Without taking the time to allow the Holy Spirit to renew your mind, whenever you may experience a temporary weakness in your faith (as we all do sometimes) and the first time the enemy brings at depressive thought to you, you will begin to doubt your healing.

It is important to understand that healing is received and maintained by **faith. God honors faith; there is no other way!**

Understand is that you were delivered and healed before you even got sick. The healing for all your soul's diseases was given when, *he was wounded for our transgressions, he was bruised for our iniquities: the chastisement of our peace was upon him; and with his stripes we are healed (Isaiah 53:2).* The healing and deliverance occurs the moment it is received in the heart of the believer. But some of us just don't have the faith to receive it. It's like walking around with strep throat, sick as a dog, with a penicillin shot in your hand. It won't do you any good until you inject it.

And so God in his infinite mercy and grace will draw us to his healing waters through his lovingkindness. He will allow us to go through until we are ready to receive our deliverance. He'll be with us, and he'll keep us from harm, but the decision to receive our healing must be ours, alone. **God honors faith.**

Too many of us want to believe God for a miracle rather than trust him to bring us through. For some situations, healing takes time, and we have just got to <u>walk it out</u>.

Get Your Joy Back!

When I was seeking the Lord for a word on the subject of restoring lost joy, he put this question in my heart;

" What did <u>you</u> want to know when you went through depression and brokenness?"

After thinking about it, I realized that I needed desperately to know four things:

1. **Am I going crazy?** God's answer: No!

For God hath not given us the spirit of fear; but of power, and of love, and of a sound mind (2Timothy 1:7).

2. **Does God really hear my call, and is he really, truly going to help me?** God's answer: Yes and Yes!

> *I sought the LORD, and he heard me, and delivered me from all my fears (.Psalm 34:10)*

3. **Does God still love me?** God's answer: Yes!

> *For I am persuaded, that neither death, nor life, nor angels, nor principalities, nor powers, nor things present, nor things to come, 39 Nor height, nor depth, nor any other creature, shall be able to separate us from the love of God, which is in Christ Jesus our Lord (Romans 8:38-39)*

2. **What does the word have to say about dealing with depression?**

In addition to a great company of Christians who have publicly admitted to having suffered from some form of depression, such as Jan Crouch, Paula White, and Joyce Meyer; there are several examples of individuals going through depressive episodes in the scriptures such as David after his sin with Bathsheba, Job after he lost everything, and Isaiah when Jezebel was after him. From these examples and others, there are seven keys outlined in the scriptures for dealing with depression, or any other kind of trouble.

I. <u>Understand that trouble is going to come. It may not last, but it will surely come.</u> Jesus said, *In the world ye shall have tribulation: but be of good cheer; I have overcome the world.(John 16:33)* If you have never had any trouble, just keep on living.

II. <u>When trouble comes, as it surely will, Have faith in God.</u> *(Mark 11:22).* Keep your eyes on Jesus, not your situation! Why, why, why do we as Christians always allow our circumstances to make us take our eyes off Jesus? Even after he has delivered us time and time again, some of us still get down the road and act like we have forgotten what God has done for us. **God honors faith.**

III. <u>Don't be afraid. Fear and intimidation are two of the enemy's most powerful weapons. If he can keep you in fear, he can keep you in bondage.</u> Remember, *God hath not given us the spirit of fear; but of power, and of love, and of a sound mind (2Timothy 1:7).* Open your mouth and say, **"I resist the spirit of fear in the name of Jesus"** every time fear tries to come upon you.

IV. <u>Confess all known sin. Unconfessed sin can hinder your prayer:</u> *If I regard iniquity in my heart, the Lord will not hear me.(Psalm 66:18)* It can also open the door to satanic attacks, so give the devil no ground.

Come clean with God. Submit yourself to him and allow him to search you and expose any hidden sin or rebellion.

V. <u>Take God at his word.</u> Ask yourself; *Is there anything too hard for God? (Genesis 18:14)* If he said he would heal and deliver you, he will. His word will not return to him void. Be honest with yourself and God about where you are in your faith. If your faith is weak, remember, you can always ask God, *help thou mine unbelief* (Mark 9:24) Then make up your mind that no matter what happens, you are going to believe God. Don't go by what you feel, hear, or even see. This is a faith journey, *For we walk by faith, not by sight (2Corinthians 5:7).*

You must receive your healing by faith.
Without faith it is impossible to please God.
(Hebrew 11:6)

VI. Expect full restoration. The bible says God
not only vindicated Job before his friends,
but *the LORD gave Job twice as much as*
he had before. (Job 42:2) **And He will do**
the same for you!

Those who sow in tears shall reap in joy.
Jesus came *to heal the brokenhearted. . .*
to give unto them beauty for ashes, the oil
of joy for mourning, the garment of praise
for the spirit of heaviness; (Isaiah 61:1-2).
You will get **all** your stuff back! And then
some. If you believe it praise him now.

VII. **Never lose your praise.** Your victory is in
your praise because this is ultimately
what the enemy is after. His plan for you
is the same as it was for Job: to have you

too sick and depressed to come to church, too sad to sing Zion songs, and too angry and hurt to acknowledge that God is worthy to be praise **just because he is God**. But when you continue to give God the praise that he is due even when your hedge of protection is gone and you are in the midst of your pain and suffering, **you get the victory!!** So keep on praising Him and when He heals you, go tell somebody. Their deliverance could be in your testimony.

GETTING TO THE NEXT LEVEL:
FASTING, PRAYER , AND AGREEMENT

-Think for a minute about what it would be like to have it all.

You drive the right car,

Live in the right neighborhood

Work on the right job, and you

Have the right mate.

You've just got it going on!

Most people probably think they'd be fairly

satisfied, but if you think that all of this would

satisfy your deepest soul longings, you would be wrong.

There would still be something missing.

You may not be able to put your finger on the cause, but you can't deny the feeling that something is missing in your life.

You are supposed to feel this way.

You are supposed to want more out of life than things. That empty spot in your soul belongs there. The problem is that many people don't understand this and they are sometimes driven to acts of self-destruction when they try to fill that emptiness. Many try to fill the void with drugs, power, sex, relationships, and money, even church work, but none of this satisfies, and it's not supposed to. **God placed that longing in your heart and only He can satisfy it.**

So here you are. Sis/Bro /Rev. /Dr. Do Right.

All righteous in your righteousness.

All holy in your holiness.

You know that you are saved and that your name is written in the Lamb's Book of Life.

You know that you know, that you know, that you are God's elect.

You go to church, pay your tithes, serve anyway you can, but still

Something is missing. The void, the empty place, the longing is still there. Maybe not as bad, but still you know it's there

You long for a closer walk, a deeper intimacy with God.

Your desire to know Him more becomes so fervent that you begin to seek after Him with all your heart.

You no longer seek him just for things, you want nothing less than His heart.

Some people say that you are a God chaser, but guess what? You don't have to chase God.

He's not running. *For the eyes of the LORD run to and fro throughout the whole earth, to shew himself strong in the behalf of them whose heart is perfect toward him.(2Chronicles 16:9).*

God wants the same intimacy with you that you desire of Him. *For the Father seeketh such to worship him. (John 4:23)*

So then the question becomes, how does one reach a deeper level of intimacy with God?

I have sought the Lord, and searched the scriptures, and I am convinced that the answer can come through "Fasting, Prayer , and Agreement." Note the order, Fasting, Prayer and Agreement." God gave me this message in that order and that is how I will teach it.

What is Fasting?

By tradition to fast means to abstain from food and /or drink for a specified period. Spiritually, fasting means exchanging the physical needs for the spiritual through the subduing of physical desires and passions while seeking God in prayer.

What the Word says about fasting

-It is an expected discipline :

Moreover, when you fast, be not as the hypocrites, of a sad countenance. (Matt. 6:16). Notice that Jesus said **when** you fast, not **if** you fast.

It is clear from his language that believers are expected fast periodically.

No set length of time or type of fast mentioned in the bible is said to be preferable to another. Some who fast simply abstain from all food and drink only water for a short period anywhere from one meal to several days. Others fast for longer periods;

Moses, Paul, and Jesus are all said to have fasted for forty days. Some people fast individually, but sometimes church leaders may call for a corporate fast. Some fasts may involve abstaining from a particular type of food such as meat. One popular fast among Christians today is the Daniel fast which mostly involves eating vegetables and drinking water for a period of ten to twenty days.(*Daniel 1:11-16*).

The point is that there are no set rules except that it be sincere:

Moreover when ye fast, be not, as the hypocrites, of a sad countenance: for they disfigure their faces, that they may appear unto men to fast. Verily I say unto you, They have their reward. 17 But thou, when thou fastest, anoint thine head, and wash thy face; 18 That thou appear not unto men to fast, but unto thy Father which is in secret: and thy Father, which seeth in secret, shall reward thee

openly.(Matthew 6"16-18).

The bottom line? When you fast, wash your face, anoint your head, and avoid looking like you are fasting. Fasting is about the condition of the heart.

Why You Should Fast

Fasting is physically, emotionally, and spiritually grueling. Your flesh will not be happy about being denied. I sometimes become nauseous, or develop a pounding headache when I am fasting. So the question is, what makes fasting worth the trouble? What does it prove? There are some who say "God knows my heart, I don't have anything to prove.' God does indeed know our hearts, but sometimes we may not until it is revealed to us through fasting.

Imagine that there were two people who professed their undying love for you. The first is one who tells you constantly, "I love you." He or she comes to see you once, sometimes twice a week, Every once in a while they will think about you, and will call to tell you this, especially when they are getting ready to ask you for something.

But the other is one who rearranges his or her life to spend time with you. They will give up their other lovers, their habits, their selfish agendas to pursue you and only you. They are determined to win your heart.

Which one would you be most likely to give your heart to?

The second lover shows an earnest desire to have you, that is somehow lacking in the first. It is not so much the persistent attention that tugs at your heart, but it is their earnest sincerity that says "I'm not playing around, I want you!"

When you fast and pray it shows God this same thing.

1. Fasting manifests and earnestness to God to the exclusion of all else. And God responds not just to the fast, but to the sincerity in your heart. Consider the story of Jehoshaphat:

It came to pass after this also, that the children of Moab, and the children of Ammon, and with them other beside the Ammonites, came against Jehoshaphat to battle. 2 Then there came some that told Jehoshaphat, saying, There cometh a great multitude against thee from beyond the sea on this side Syria; and, behold, they be in Hazazontamar, which is Engedi. 3 And Jehoshaphat feared, Surrounded by the enemy and facing the possibility of a losing battle, Jehoshaphat did what everyone should do in such a situation, *he set himself to seek the LORD, and proclaimed a fast throughout all Judah.*

The whole nation fasted and sought the Lord in prayer, *And all Judah stood before the LORD, with their little ones, their wives, and their children,* The Lord heard their prayers and responded to the earnest fast through Jahaziel:

Thus saith the LORD unto you, Be not afraid nor dismayed by reason of this great multitude; for the battle is not yours, but God's (2Chr 20:1-4)

If you really want to show God that you want His heart, do like Jehoshaphat, try seeking him through fasting and prayer.

3. Fasting humbles the soul

I humbled my soul through fasting. . Ps. 35:13

By denying fleshly appetites the soul is chastened and humbled. We are made to realize that *man doth not live by bread only, but by every word that proceedeth out of the mouth of the LORD doth man live (Dt. 8:3)*

The Lord allowed the murmuring Israelites to go hungry, then he fed them with manna so that they would learn this very thing (Dt. 8:1-3).

It is God who supplies our needs; He is our source.

4. **Through fasting we learn total dependence on God.**

When I am on a particularly grueling fast, each pang of hunger, or moment or physical weakness reminds me that God is the source of my strength. The more weak and hungry I feel, the more I am forced to think about the Lord until I finally reach a point that am walking in the full awareness of his caring , sustaining presence in my life. It is truly a humbling experience.

When one humbles himself before God through fasting or any other method, he is saying: "Without you Lord, I am nothing." Isaiah 57:15 reminds us,

For thus saith the high and lofty One that inhabiteth eternity, whose name is Holy; I dwell in the high and

holy place, with him also that is of a contrite and

humble spirit, to revive the spirit of the humble, and

to revive the heart of the contrite ones

**When our spirits are humbled through fasting,
the Holy Spirit is able to reveal to us our true
spiritual condition.** As we stand, humbled, and
spiritually naked before God, He begins to expose
unconfessed sin, and unyielded areas in our lives.
Some things about ourselves we simply are not
ready to acknowledge or accept, and we cannot
repent of them until we do. For example, I have
always considered myself a selfless, giving person.
Through fasting, I learned that, like most people, I
can indeed be very selfish. Not only did God show
me the selfish thoughts and motives behind some
of my 'caring' words and actions, He even revealed
the pride hidden behind such thinking . I was
appalled. Sometimes those of us who consider
ourselves righteous can seriously delude ourselves

about our faults and the level of sin in our lives; fasting can be a painful reminder that we are still human, still sinners saved by grace, and still in need of God's mercy.

Once these areas are revealed, confessed, and repented of, **fasting moves you into a spiritual realm that enables you to hear from God.**

The book of Acts records an incident in which fasting helped bring the answer to a prayer: *Cornelius said, Four days ago I was fasting until this hour; and at the ninth hour I prayed in my house, and, behold, a man stood before me in bright clothing, 31 And said, Cornelius, thy prayer is heard, and thine alms are had in remembrance in the sight of God. (Acts 10:30)*

The Relationship Between Fasting and Prayer

In almost all of the Biblical examples given here, Fasting went hand in hand with prayer. Fasting puts down the power of our flesh and thereby intensifies our focus on God. The earnestness of fasting and fervent, heartfelt prayer is a powerful combination that God will not ignore. If you really want to seek the face and know the heart of God, fasting and prayer cant take you into his very presence.

What is prayer?

The word prayer comes from the Greek word 'proseuche' meaning communion with God. Prayer is not just words, or meaningless repetitions .

Christ warns us against this, *But when ye pray, use not vain repetitions, as the heathen do: for they think that they shall be heard for their much speaking. Matt 6:7)*

Prayer is seeking a heartfelt relationship with God. It is not an exchange system to receive things from God. Prayer is an acknowledgment of the worthiness of God to be praised because of what He has done and for who He is, the creator and sustainer of the universe. (If He never does anything else, he is and will always be worthy.) Prayer is the lifting your heart to God's heart in a joining of spirits.

God inhabits the praise of his people.

Forms of prayer

Prayer can take many forms. Some are prayers of **confession** like the publican in the book of Luke:

God be merciful to me a sinner   Luke 18:13

Some prayers are **petitions** to God for help with a problem or issue like Jehoshaphat's prayer:

O our God, wilt thou not judge them? for we have no might against this great company that cometh against us; neither know we what to do: but our eyes are upon thee.(2Chr. 20:12)

Often in our prayers we **intercede** or stand in the gap for others. The Holy Spirit is continually making intercession for us even as we pray; He will also teach us how to pray: *for we know not what we should pray for as we ought: but the Spirit itself maketh intercession for us with groanings which* *cannot be uttered. 27 And he that searcheth the hearts knoweth what is the mind of the Spirit, because he maketh intercession for the saints according to the will of God (Romans 8:26-27)*

Intercessory prayer can be a powerful weapon against the enemy; therefore, in addition to interceding and standing in the gap for others, we should also pray for the nations, and the peace of Jerusalem. An incident recorded in the book of Ezekiel explains the importance of intercessory prayer:

*Thus saith the Lord GOD, when the LORD hath not spoken. 29 The people of the land have used oppression, and exercised robbery, and have vexed the poor and needy: yea, they have oppressed the stranger wrongfully. 30 And I sought for a man among them, that should make up the hedge, and **stand in the gap before me** for the land, that I should not destroy it: but I found none. 31 Therefore* *have I poured out mine indignation upon them.*

Ezekiel 22:29-31).

If one man had prayed, God would not have destroyed the land. We should always pray for our nation.

There are some who pray **in the spirit and with other tongues:**

I will pray with the spirit, and I will pray with the understanding also. (1 Cor. 14:13-14)

No matter what kind of prayer we pray or how we pray it, the bible reminds us that , *It is a good thing to give thanks unto the LORD, and to sing praises unto thy name, O most High,(Psalm 92:1).*

This is the **prayer of praise and worship;** it can change the entire atmosphere.

I have often heard it said that 'when praises go up, blessings come down.' It sounds pretty and we love to say things that sound 'spiritual.' But read what really happens when praises go up:

*And it came to pass, when the priests were come out of the holy place: (for all the priests that were present were sanctified, and did not then wait by course: 12 Also the Levites which were the singers, all of them of Asaph, of Heman, of Jeduthun, with their sons and their brethren, being arrayed in white linen, having cymbals and psalteries and harps, stood at the east end of the altar, and with them an hundred and twenty priests sounding with trumpets:) 13 It came even to pass, as the trumpeters and singers were as one, to make one sound to be heard in praising and thanking the LORD; and when they lifted up their voice with the trumpets and cymbals and instruments of music, and praised the LORD, saying, For he is good; for his mercy endureth for ever: that then the house was filled with a cloud, even the house of the LORD; 14 So that the priests could not stand to minister by reason of the cloud: **for the glory of the LORD had***

filled the house of God. *(2 Chron 5:11-14)*

<u>God inhabits the praise of his people.</u> When praise and worship go up, the Shekinah Glory (the glory of His presence) of God comes down, and you find yourself in the very presence of God.

The prayer of praise and worship is not just a chance for you to bless God, it is a chance for him to bless you! **Always and in everything, praise ye the Lord.**

Agreement : The Power of Unified Prayer

The book of Matthew explains the power of unified prayer:

Again I say unto you, That if two of you shall agree on earth as touching any thing that they shall ask, it shall be done for them of my Father which is in heaven. 20 For where two or three are gathered together in my name, there am I in the midst of them. (Matthew 18:19)

As you can see, when two or more agree in prayer, there is always another silent prayer in the person of Jesus Christ. The most compelling example of the power of unified prayer can be found

In the book of Acts: *And when the day of Pentecost was fully come, they were all with one accord in one place Acts 1: 1*

The disciples were all In one place, on one accord; none were unconcerned, uninterested, or lukewarm. All were earnest and united in faith and prayer.

<u>The result: the birth of the New Testament Church!</u>

Imagine yoking up with someone who is on one accord with you, united in faith and prayer. In agreement with you. The spiritual power of fasting and praying in agreement are virtually limitless, and if you allow Him, God will prove it the day you unite in prayer and fasting with someone else.

Three things you should always do before praying or agreeing with someone in prayer.

1. Confess all known sin. If *we confess our sins, he is faithful and just to forgive us our sins, and to cleanse us from all unrighteousness. (1John:1:9)*

2. Forgive all who have hurt or offended you And when ye stand praying, forgive, if ye have ought against any: that your Father also which is in heaven may forgive you your trespasses. 26 But if ye do not forgive, neither will your Father which is in heaven forgive your trespasses. (Mark 11:25-26)

3. Submit your heart to be searched by God and acknowledge what he reveals to you. God knows what is in your heart. *The spirit of man is the candle of the LORD, searching all the inward parts of the belly.(Proverbs 20:27)*

Preparation for Prayer

- Quiet your mind and wait in God's presence so you can feel God's heart and pray the things the Holy Spirit shows you to pray for.

- Have the word of God in your heart and in your mouth. Pray according to his word which is his will. *So shall my word be that goeth forth out of my mouth: it shall not return unto me void, but it shall accomplish that which I please, and it shall prosper in the thing whereto I sent it. (Is. 55:11)*

- Pray in faith. *Let us hold fast the profession of our faith without wavering; (for he is faithful that promised;) (Heb. 10: 23)*

- If you have doubt in your heart, ask God to heal your unbelief.

- Only choose someone to agree with you who truly has the same or greater level of faith that you do, and are on one accord with you.

- Use your power of attorney. Ask in the name of Jesus. *And whatsoever ye shall ask in my name, that will I do, that the Father may be glorified in the Son. 14 If ye shall ask any thing in my name, I will do it. (John 14: 13-14)*

A Word About "Unanswered" Prayer

There is no such thing. I believe God answers all sincere prayer. The answer may not be what we want to hear. It may not be what we expect. It may not even be what we asked for. But it will always be what is best whether we understand it or not.

For a long time, I thought that I had to understand what God was doing in every situation. If I, or someone I loved was going through something, I would pray with great assurance that God would hear and answer.

If my prayers were not answered according to my desires, I would rationalize until I came up with an acceptable reason that God would deny me. It would usually be something like, "Well, God has something better for me."

How foolish I was! Our thoughts are not his thoughts. Our ways are not his ways:

For as the heavens are higher than the earth, so are my ways higher than your ways, and my thoughts than your thoughts. Isaiah 55: 9

The truth is, **God owes us no explanations**. <u>**We simply have to trust him.**</u>

I learned the truth of this statement through a situation that began when my son was a toddler, and his father and I went through an ugly divorce. I was working as an RN at the time, and I was so stressed that I was barely functional.

I needed time to regroup, so I happily accepted my sister Cherry's invitation to visit her in Ft. Leonard Wood, Missouri, where her husband was stationed.

When I got there, she told me that her youngest daughter was struggling with her schoolwork, and she confided that the child's teacher had asked her to consider letting her remain in kindergarten another year instead of going to the first grade because she could not read. Cherry knew her daughter was bright, (all of her children are) and she kept a ready supply of books and educational toys in her home.

Each evening during the two weeks that I was there, I would work with the child using a simple reward system and some Dr. Seuss books. I would read a page to her, and reward her with a Froot Loop or an M&M each time she successfully read the page back to me. It was fun for her, and it gave me an opportunity to think of something besides my own problems. And it created a lasting bond between the two of us.

A few weeks after I returned home, my sister called me, hardly able to contain her excitement. It seemed that her daughter had taken to books like a fish to water and was now reading everything she could get her hands on. Not only did she do well in kindergarten, she excelled academically the rest of her life. My first pupil ended up receiving accolade upon accolade for her academic talent. We eventually lost count of the scholarships and awards she received during her college years.

That child was Regan Robinson, my niece who was just a few months shy of graduating from medical school when she died of colon cancer in 2006, leaving a bewildered and completely devastated family.

I do not pretend to understand why Regan died so young, newly married, and full of promise, although I spent months trying to do just that.

If prayer could have saved her, I believe she would be yet alive.

I don't understand, **but I trust God**. And while I don't understand her death, I do understand her life. She had a heart that was as close to perfect toward God as I believe one can achieve on this side of heaven. God may not have healed Regan as she prayed, and in the manner we desired, but she died believing that he could. Her life was an inspiration and a blessing to so many people, some of whom she never got to meet.

I am one of the many lives that were changed by the beautiful life of this remarkable young woman. Through Regan, I discovered my gift for teaching and it altered the entire course of my life.

I eventually left the nursing field and became the teacher I know God created me to be.

From the brokenness of divorce came the beauty of touching and being touched by the earth angel that was Regan Robinson Young.

This is the point: When you pray, **trust God**. No matter what. Even when you don't understand, trust God. He knows you intimately, loves you unconditionally, **and He always has your best interest at heart.**

Sold Out To Jesus

Some people may wonder what it means to be 'sold out' to Jesus. For me, it means being in a place of complete surrender to God. It means letting go of the world and embracing the things of God with all that is in you. **It means you have made up your mind to follow Jesus and no matter what happens on your journey, <u>turning back is not an option</u>** because there is nothing to turn back to that can offer you what Jesus offers.

One of the best ways to explain what it means to be sold out to Jesus is through the story of the potter's wheel:

The word which came to Jeremiah from the LORD, saying, 2 Arise, and go down to the potter's house, and there I will cause thee to hear my words. 3 Then I went down to the potter's house, and, behold, he wrought a work on the wheels. (That **work** is you and me)

4 And the vessel that he made of clay was marred in the hand of the potter: so he made it again another vessel, as seemed good to the potter to make it. (Jeremiah 18:1-4)

This marring represents our mess-ups, our slip ups, our sins, spots, and blemishes. I don't know about anyone else, but when I first got saved, I didn't always do what I was supposed to do. I went places I wasn't supposed to go, and I kept some company that I wasn't supposed to keep. There were still some areas in my life that I had not fully surrendered to God, **and my head was as hard as a brick!**

I thought I knew it all. But I am so glad that God does not throw us away when we mess up. Instead, like the potter, He takes us into his loving hands, breaks us down, puts us back on the wheel and continues the lifelong process of molding and making us after his will. Every now and then, God, in his infinite mercy, will still break me down, put me back on that wheel, and begin a new work in me.

In my lifetime, I have been on that wheel many times, whining and complaining, and wondering why in the world God was allowing these things to happen to me. But as I look back on my experiences, I realize that with each turn of the wheel, God was shaping me, forming me, preparing me, toughening me, and instilling character and integrity in me so that I could be a vessel fit for the master's use. **These experiences kept me at his mercy; they taught me to call on Jesus and to trust him no matter what.**

While I was on that wheel, something happened to me. Even in our earthly relationships, trials bring closeness. Two people whom I call best friends, Ivon and Emily, earned that distinction because they have walked with me through my fiery trials. Whenever I find myself looking through the flames of trials, one of them is always there. This same thing is what happened in my relationship with God. No matter how bad things got, no matter how low in spirit I sank, **<u>I could always feel God's presence, and I knew I was not alone.</u>** When I looked back, I realized that through it all, the one person who was always there, who never deserted me, who comforted me when nothing else would, was God. Just like He was in that fiery furnace with those Hebrew boys, God went through every one of my fiery trials with me. And He did this for one very simple reason; <u>He loves me. Totally, completely, and unconditionally, God loves me. He may not love everything that I do, but He loves me.</u> You just have to have been where I've been to understand what a life-changing revelation that was for somebody like me.

I didn't even love myself!

But God was like a persistent suitor; **he courted my heart, and he pursued me until he won it.** I don't know why He loved me so much, but I love Him because He first loved me. I learned to love Him not only for what He has done, but just for who He is. It was God's love for me that made me surrender my heart and my life to him, and become completely sold out to Jesus. I encourage you to trust God, no matter what you may be going through. His message to you today is that **you are not alone**. <u>**God is with you.**</u>

He hears your cry and he pities your every groan. When your are going through a bad situation, I encourage you to stay on the wheel and let God complete that good work he has begun in you. He wants nothing less than your whole heart and he will never stop pursuing you until you too, are **Sold Out to Jesus.**

www.ingramcontent.com/pod-product-compliance
Lightning Source LLC
Chambersburg PA
CBHW051811040426
42446CB00007B/615